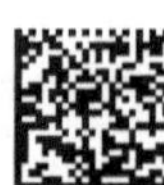
www.ingramcontent.com/pod-product-compliance
Lightning Source LLC
Chambersburg PA
CBHW051508030726
47592CB00006B/2150

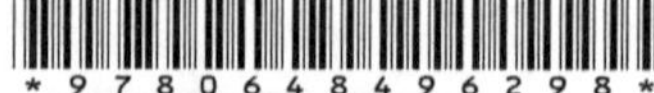

200

table of contents